90 Days

to Your Success

How to create success in your life –

90 days at a time.

The Complete Planning and Execution
Tool for Building Your Business

Manny Nowak

Dedication

This book is dedicated to my family. The real success in my life. I thank God each day for them and the joy they bring to my life.

Thanks to my clients who have been using the 90 days process, both formally and informally over many years. It has taken a great deal of trial and error to get it working as smooth and effectively as it is. It has helped many of them to move their businesses to new levels of success. But they have also helped me in being able to help so many more of you. Thank you.

Enjoy this book and may it help you to take your life to new levels of success. Coach Manny Nowak

Manny@MannyNowak.com

www.CoachManny.com

CONTENTS

DISCLAIMER

international, federal, state, and local governing professional licensing, business practices, advertising, and all other aspects of doing business in the US, Canada, or any other jurisdiction is the sole responsibility of the purchaser or reader. Neither the author nor the publisher assumes any responsibility or liability whatsoever on the behalf of the purchaser or reader of these materials. Any perceived slight of any individual or organization is purely unintentional. I sometimes use affiliate links in the content. This means if you decide to make a purchase, I will get a sales commission. But that doesn't mean my opinion is for sale. Every affiliate link on is to products that I've personally used and found useful. Please do your own research before making any purchase online.

Chapter 1 – Overview of the Process

The only real capital is time, but it is capital only when used.

Napoleon Hill

The 90 days to success process is a new way of looking at your life. Up to this point you might have been working with what people call "planning" for the next year. That process has been around forever, and it is based on asking you to look at the next year and figure out what it is you are going to accomplish over that year and how you are going to do it. Then you put together goals and tasks to accomplish those goals over the next year.

Trouble is that a year in today's world is a long time.

For some a very long time.

This can lead us to putting things off, procrastination.

In the world of planning that can many times mean we have all the great intention to get things done and work them all year long, but just like those term papers in high school, we wait until the last minute to do them. Thus what happens is we don't do as great a job as we could have.

Yearly planning processes are what leads us to get so much done in the 4th quarter.

It is why we work so hard in that last 3 months to bring home stuff, that we should have been working all along.

But more so, it is why we get to goal, but usually do not far exceed it.

Just think about what would happen if you worked that hard all year long?

You see, you just get it done and do it well, but what if you had of started and finished it earlier, how much better could it have been.

Doing this reach really kick off a spark in my mind and I got really inspired to build this process.

The key to success with this process is teaching yourself to look at life in 3 month pieces as opposed to 12 months.

The payback you will quickly realize is that you can get your hands around the process of 90 days so much easier.

Now when it comes to execution, this process, in some ways it is harder because you have to move so much faster.

You have so much less time to get things done.

But if you have been following my stuff over the years, then you know that you use the time you allocate and you get the job done. Give yourself less time, and you will still get it done.

In most ways, the success you achieve is so worth the journey and actually the results can be so much greater if you follow the process.

Whether you are in sales, production, operations, finance or any other department out there, this process works. This process will create amazing results for you whether you work for someone else or for yourself.

Just take a moment and remember what happens in corporate America today.

We spend months putting together a plan for next year.

Then what happens is that most of the success actually happens in the final 90 days of the year. This is when push comes to shove.

What if you had that 4th quarter mentality all year long?

Get your hands around that and you will understand this process.

One word of caution.

This is not a short term solution that ignores the long-term.

I know some of you may be thinking this is just like so much short-term thinking in America today. I only care about today. This is actually just short term execution, but long term thinking as you will see in the first part.

We start thinking very long term, but when it comes to execution, we are always in a 90 day window.

Chapter 2 - Building the Long-Term Process

Chapter Objective: Define and Write your long-term objectives.

Face the worst,

Believe the best.

Do the most.

Leave the rest.

Bishop Mel Wheatley

Before we look at your 90-day plan, we start the process by looking out far into the future.

This is a method that will help you start thinking long-term and then focus in to the next 90 days.

Here is what we want you to think about to start with:

30 Years out.

20 Years out.

10 years out.

5 years out.

3 years out.

1 year out.

90 days out.

For each of the above I want you to define where you see yourself and write the answers to the following questions:

1/   What am I going to be doing?

2/   Where am I at this point in life?

3/   What does life look like?

Starting with 30 years and answer the questions.

Please do not pass over this piece. It makes you really think, which is why the process works. It is like planning to walk from New York City to Los Angeles. You have to have a plan, a map and goals for each day to get there. The long term is Los Angles, but to get there I have to first get out of the city of New York.

Then based on your answers for 30 years, where do you have to be in 20 years to make that happen.

Then continue to the next time frame , ask yourself, to get there, where do I have to be in 10, 5,3 and 1 years, respectively.

You will be amazed at how this process makes you think outside the norm.

Note: If 70 or over, use 100 minus your age for the top time frame.

If 30 or younger, go out 50 years.

If you are anywhere in between, adjust as you see fit.

I want you to think about the furthest point so you can walk backwards.

The biggest problem with most people is they spend more time planning their wedding and their vacations than they do planning their life and their career.

Plus, most of us think too short term.

Yes, the 90-day process is focused short term, but the goals are always what you need to accomplish in the short-term to get to your long-term dreams. It is walking a step at a time in the right direction with the ladder against the right building.

If you think about where you want to be 30+ years from now, you will be way past there when the time comes.

This process will get you to work(execute) in 90 day windows but think in decades.

Here is an example to help you get a feel for this process.

Long-Term Goal Sheet

30 Years out.

What am I going to be doing?

Writing books and advising others. Giving my money away. Still walking on the beach every day

Where am I at this point in life?

Living on the beach where it is warm

What does life look like?

Coming to a close but I am still healthy and doing well. All the money me and my family will ever need

20 Years out.

What am I going to be doing?

Writing speaking and selling great stuff. Still making excellent money and giving much of it away.

Where am I at this point in life?

Living at the beach

What does life look like?

Enjoying each day and the people in my family Children, grandchildren great grandchildren.

10 years out.

What am I going to be doing?

Hit the goal of 10 million dollars. Still doing high level consulting at excellent rates. Company is creating most of that revenue through events and product sales.

Where am I at this point in life?

Heavy accumulation finished, turning over day to day to next person. Moving back to doing writing and speaking more than anything else

What does life look like?

Life is looking great. Still working 3 days a week and growing a multimillion dollar operation

5 years out.

What am I going to be doing?

Building the internal team that can take over all the stuff I don't want to do. Putting the right people on the bus. Over $3 million in sales at this point

Where am I at this point in life?

Loving what I do, but delegating as much as I can buy getting the right players in.

What does life look like?

Money is not really an issue

3 years out.

What am I going to be doing?

Second year in a row over 1 million in sales. Working hard but not long. 3 days a week.

Where am I at this point in life?

Money is starting to come in from sources other than me

What does life look like?

4 days at beach

1 year out.

What am I going to be doing?

All in place to hit 1 million in next 12 months. Building major new and repurposed product. Selling major amounts of product through speaking and live video.

Where am I at this point in life?

Enjoying the hustle and growth. Building a few key players in the organization.

What does life look like?

All the pieces in place to work 3 days a week effectively.

90 Days

What am I going to be doing?

90 days to success is rolling out and starting to sell

Where am I at this point in life?

Building and selling and speaking

What does life look like?

Growing the company and ready to start putting new players on.

Chapter 3 -Setting Your Goals.

Chapter Objective: Write your goals for the next 90 days.

What the mind conceives and believes it can achieve.

William Clement

Goals that you will accomplish in the next 90 days. Write

them here and remember Use SMART –

Specific – be very direct in what it is, not vague.

Measurable – countable, I can measure the results.

Achievable – you have to believe you can do this.

Relevant – it has to be on target for your long-term, or why are you doing it.

Time limited – when will it be done. How much time. Start/end.

The next thing we will be working on is to set your goals for the first 90-day process.

Here is a list of the standard categories and also one for "other" in case we missed something that is important to you. Please take a moment and review these.

Business – your business, your job. If stay at home mom or dad – that is your job.

Personal – for you. This includes self-development and things you want to do for you.

Financial – money.

Home – your house car other physical possessions.

Family – those you love

Faith – religion what you believe.

Health – keeping you at top shape.

Other – any category you need that we did not fit into.

You do not have to do each category when you start, or ever in fact. You might even add one I do not have. (please send me note if you do so I can add to the goal worksheet.) We suggest you start with just your business for the first 90 days and see how you do with it. Then you can add a few or all of your goals as you move forward. But I know some of you super achievers will want to do them all at once, so have at it.

Second, it is very important that you do not create too many goals. As we all know from past experience that if this process becomes more work than it is worth, you will not do it. So many times, in my work of sales automation we find that certain things are better left manual.

1/   You should have no more than 2-4 business goals, the less the better.

2/   No more than 12 goals overall.

3/   Your key is to make it happen not to create a super plan.

4/   If it doesn't get executed, it is not worth much.

Here is an example of goals for your review:

1/   Remember this is for the next 90 days only. You will achieve these.

2/   These goals must help you accomplish your long-term goals.

Business

Generate 200K in income

Implement the new ABC CRM system.

Hire a full-time sales rep.

Personal

Read 3 books

Play golf twice a month.

Financial

Pay off credit card 123.

Home

Get deck painted.

Hire person to mow the lawn and get them started.

Family

Spend Sundays with my family doing things together.

Pay off vacation trip for summer.

Faith

Read my daily devotional book every morning and the scripture that goes with it.

Health

Walk 200 miles

Other

Tip:

Example has 12 goals in it.

This is good.

Going to much above this makes it very hard to manage. I know you are a superstar, but please limit your total number of goals to a manageable level..

Assignment:

Your task is now to write your goals for the next 90 days.

If you are in the middle of the month, then make them start next month.

It is best to start at the beginning of a month.

If you are in a few days, it is ok to back date them.

This is very critical foundation to your 90 days success goal.

You should not rush it or wing it.

You can use the attached spreadsheet, or you can us the following word sheet and write them.

90 Days to Success

Goal Sheet

My Goals for the next 90 days:

Name:

Period start date:

Period end date:

Business

Personal

Financial

Home

Family

Faith

Health

Other

Keeping you Sharp:

Now that you have developed the goals, the next step is to write these goals out by hand twice every day. Yes, I understand you might have some objection, but this is a very proven process and it works.

I did not come up with it.

I just use it and teach it.

I personally write my goals each morning and every evening.

You need to write your goals twice every day.

Handwritten on a piece of paper.

This is a great process that was first taught to me by Brian Tracy many years ago. It has further been proven by many others. There is a hand/mind connection that happens when you do this critical success step.

You need to write your goals once when you get up and once before you go to sleep.

Key:

Not once in a while but ***every single day***.

Yes, it seems wild, crazy.

You might even be saying, "Are you kidding me?"

I am not, this is so important.

Writing your goals out by hand every morning and evening will ingrain them into your head and you will be amazed at what happens when you do it.

Every day – twice

You now know what you want to accomplish and now it is simply time to do it.

Chapter 4 - Defining the Tasks For Those Goals

Chapter Objective: Define and write the tasks that will make your goals happen.

Both poverty and riches are the offspring of thought.

Napoleon Hill

Tasks

Now for each goal you have set, you need to define the "what?"

What are the tasks that you have to do in order to make this goal happen?

This is so key to your success and in making this process work for you.

So many people each year make New Year resolutions, only to break them very soon after the new year. In fact, I have heard numbers as high as 90% by end of January and then ½ of the remaining number break them by the end of March.

This must be where we get the 5% people from. That 5% this are making it happen in the world today.

I actually don't believe it is 5%, I believe the number really is only 2%.

You are part of that 2% - so keep on rolling.

What you need to do in this step of the process is define in detail, what tasks you are going to have to do in order to make each goal a reality.

Remember that goals are easy to set and also very easy not to follow. (Part of why you write them twice a day, so you recommit to them.)

Your tasks bring goals closer to reality.

You can see what you have to do and what it is going to take to achieve each goal (right up front).

Sometimes it actually can discourage people and make them turn away when they see what is involved.   But not you, you are part of the 2%.

However, it is good to see what is actually involved in making each goal happen.

It opens your eyes.

I would rather you review and go back and potentially eliminate some of your goals at this point, than to get down the road and start to see what is involved.

Remember, when looking out 90 you can really much better understand what has to be done.

Do not be afraid to go back and actually change or even eliminate some of the goals because you have determined it just cannot be done in this window.

You might review the tasks and determine you have to cut back or cut out some of the goals.

Instead of 100K in sales, you might say 80K in sales is all I can accomplished based on what I know right now.

Instead of getting the system up and hiring new sales person, you might choose only one or the other leaving you time to make it happen – for sure and correctly.

Make sure you take your time here; this is where the rubber hits the road.

This is where you make it happen.

If you can see it here, you can make it happen out there.

Take each goal separately and define all the tasks you know you need to do to make this happen.

Group the tasks to make them easier to plan and easier to execute.

Get to the detail level that works for you. Everyone has a different level of detail they need in order to feel comfortable, do not ignore this piece.

This is your plan.

 These are things you are going to look at each week when you define and schedule what you are going to be doing.

After the first or second 90 day period you will have a better idea of what makes this process work for you.

It is a consistent learning process.

Let's look at an example

Goals with Tasks:

Business

Goal: Generate 200K in income

Tasks: Execute 12 interviews for the weekly podcast.

Do a Facebook live training session every week.

Spend $500 a month on Facebook advertising.

Do 4 emails a month focused on selling courses.

Add 500 people a month to the email list funnel.

Schedule and hold two 1v1 meetings a week with prospective clients.

Send articles to 1 publication a week

Send out 10 speaking requests a week

Do 2 emails about free courses a month

Write every day for 1 hour

Put together plan for new sales rep

Manage new sales rep's work

Goal: Implement the new ABC CRM system.

Tasks: Set up the system, get all generic data for set up loaded.

Load all existing client and prospect data into the new system.

Train all team members on the system.

Begin using the system for daily sales activity by 45 days in this period.

Answer questions and build a FAQ document.

Build a tick to help you work faster.

Get the sales team trained on the process.

Get the sales team using the system.

Goal: Hire a full-time sales rep.

Tasks: Put the ad out on the website and social media

Put the word out to people we know that we are looking.

Review the resumes.

Schedule phone interviews, 15 minutes with all people we want to look at.

Schedule in person interviews with all those that pass the first test.

Define our expectations of the sales rep

Ask them about their expectations of the company.

Share what we expect.

Do personality testing

Make offer if we have viable candidate, if not, go back to step one.

Hire rep

Begin training process in our methods and process.

Team up with existing rep

Get them ready to hit hard in the next 90 days – put their 90 day plan together.

Personal

Goal: Read 3 books

Find and acquire 3 books to read.

Read 20 minutes every day.

Goal: Play golf twice a month.

Tasks: Schedule golf at start of each month.

Execute.

Financial

Goal: Pay off credit card 123.

Tasks: Review balance.

Divide into 3 pieces

Pay each months current bill and the extra piece.

Home

Goal: Get deck painted.

Tasks: Get the paint

Powerwash the deck.

Paint the deck.

Goal: Hire person to mow the lawn and get them started.

Put word out to friends that I am looking.

Review ads

Call and talk with at least 5 people on the phone.

Pick 2 best to come out and talk with us.

Define the expectations we have of them and them of us.

Hire and get started if one meets our needs.

Otherwise, go back to step one.

Family

Goal: Spend Sundays with my family doing things together.

Tasks: Attend church together in the morning.

2 times attend a sporting event – professional or other.

1 visit to amusement park.

1 visit to museum.

8 times just enjoy each other and being home – play together.

Have dinner together at home or out depending on the schedule.

Relax and enjoy the evening together.

Goal: Pay off vacation trip for summer.

Tasks: Divide balance by 3.

Make 3 payments one at the start of each month.

Faith

Goal: Read my daily devotional book every morning and the scripture that goes with it.

Tasks: Get up 30 minutes early each day.

Read, pray and relax with God's Word.

Health

Goal: Walk 200 miles

Tasks: Target minimum walk of 2 miles a day.

Walk 3 miles on weekends or days where you have extra time.

Make sure 1 mile at a time for rain and days unable to make it.

Other

Assignment:

Ok, so there you have the definition.

There you have an example.

Now it is time to take your goals and put the tasks behind them.

Understand:

      that they do not have to be in order right now.

      that you might miss some.

      that you are not perfect.

Just take your goal sheet as I did above and put your task on the sheet.

Remember that tasks have to be something you can do and something you can clearly measure when they are done.

Chapter 5 - Measurements and Tracking

Chapter Objective: Define and write the measurements and tracking needed to make this happen for you.

You can't achieve great things when you leave so many things half done. Finish or dump.

Coach Manny Nowak

Now that you have your goals and the tasks ready, you need only one more thing.

You need to put it all together and add measurements and tracking.

How are you going to keep track of what you are doing?

How are you going to count the successes?

How are you going to measure?

This next section is in setting this up, so it is easy to work.

Remember a key to the 90-day success process is easy.

Go through and see what can be measured and how you can measure the goal and the tasks.

You may find you cannot measure it, so ask yourself how you are going to know it if happened?

You may add and remove stuff during this phase.

Key Point: This is a working model. It will change a great deal during the process. That is OK. Even if you have been doing this for a long time, it still will change. Sometimes I believe the more we do it, the more it keeps changing because of all we have learned.

Example Measurements and tracking:

Again, we go back to our example and show you how we implement this piece.

Goals with Tasks:

Business

Goal: Generate 200K in income (Hit the number and plot on chart)

Chart: 200k

150k

100k

50k

25K

Tasks: Execute 12 interviews for the weekly podcast. (Hit the number)

1/

2/

3/

4/

5/

6/

7/

8/

9/

10/

11/

12/

Do a Facebook live training session every week. (Check off you did it each week)

1/

2/

3/

4/

5/

6/

7/

8/

9/

10/

11/

12/

Spend $500 a month on Facebook advertising. (Hit the number)

	Projected	Actual
Month 1	500	
Month 2	500	
Month 3	500	

Do 4 emails a month focused on selling courses. (check off each time)

Month 1	1
	2
	3
	4
Month 2	1
	2
	3
	4
Month 3	1
	2
	3
	4

Add 500 people a month to the email list funnel.(track the number by month)

	Projected	Actual
Month 1	500	
Month 2	500	
Month 3	500	

Schedule and hold two 1v1 meetings a week with prospective clients.

Week	Meeting with
1	
2	
3	
4	
5	
6	

7

8

9

10

11

12

Send articles to 1 publication a week (track by week)

1

2

3

4

5

6

7

8

9

10

11

12

Send out 10 speaking requests a week (track by week that it is done)

1

2

3

4

5

6

7

8

9

10

11

12

Do 2 emails about free courses a month

	Projected	Actual
Month 1	2	
Month 2	2	
Month 3	2	

Write every day for 1 hour (use a calendar and "X" off every day you do it)

Put together plan for new sales rep (Note when you finish it)

Manage new sales rep's work (This is one I think we will drop at this point)

Goal: Implement the new ABC CRM system.

Tasks: Set up the system, get all generic data for set up loaded.

(Note when finished)

Load all existing client and prospect data into the new system.

(Note when finished)

Train all team members on the system.

(Note when finished)

Begin using the system for daily sales activity by 45 days in this period.

(Note when finished)

Answer questions and build a FAQ document.

(Note when finished)

Build a tricks to help you work faster.

(Note when finished)

Get the sales team trained on the process.

(Note when finished)

Get the sales team using the system.

(Note when Finished)

Goal: Hire a full-time sales rep.

Tasks: Put the ad out on the website and social media

(Note when finished)

Put the word out to people we know that we are looking.

(Note when finished)

Review the resumes.

(Note when finished)

Schedule phone interviews, 15 minutes with all people we want to look at.

Date   Time   Interview person

Schedule in person interviews with all those that pass the first test.

Date   Time   Interview person

Define our expectations of the sales rep

Expectations defined:

1/

2

3/

4/

5/

6/

7/

8/

9/

10/

Ask them about their expectations of the company.

Expectations they have of the company

1/

2/

3/

4/

5/

6/

7/

8/

9/

10/

Share what we expect.

(Note when done).

Do personality testing

Candidate: Results Acceptable?

Make offer if we have viable candidate, if not, go back to step one.

(Note if hired or have to return to step 1)

Hire rep

(Note name and when done)

Begin training process in our methods and process.

(Date training began)

Team up with existing rep

(Date began and who teamed up with)

Get them ready to hit hard in the next 90 days – put their 90 day plan together.

(Note when done)

Personal

Goal: Read 3 books

Tasks: Find and acquire 3 books to read.

Title   Started   Finished

1/

2/

3/

Read 20 minutes every day.

(Tick off on your calendar every day you do it)

(or put calendar in here)

Goal: Play golf twice a month.

Tasks: Schedule golf at start of each month.

Month 1:

Date Scheduled Played

1

2

Month 2:

    Date Scheduled Played

1

2

Month 3:

    Date Scheduled Played

1

2

Execute.

    (Note when all 6 rounds done)

Financial

Goal: Pay off credit card 123.

Tasks: Review balance.

Divide into 3 pieces

Pay each month's current bill and the extra piece.

Home

Goal: Get deck painted.

Tasks: Get the paint

(Note when done)

Power wash the deck.

(note when done)

Paint the deck.

Start date:

Complete Date:

Goal: Hire person to mow the lawn and get them started.

Tasks: Put word out to friends that I am looking.

(Note when done)

Review ads

(note when done)

Call and talk with at least 5 people on the phone.

1/

2/

3/

4/

5/

Pick 2 best to come out and talk with us.

1/

2/

Define the expectations we have of them and them of us.

Our expectations:

1/

2/

3/

4/

5/

6/

7/

8/

9/

10/

Their expectations of us.

1/

2/

3/

4/

5/

Hire and get started if one meets our needs.

(note when done)

Otherwise, go back to step one.

(Note if have to be done)

Family

Goal: Spend Sunday's with my family doing things together.

Tasks: Attend church together in the morning.

1/

2/

3/

4/

5/

6/

7/

8/

9/

10/

11/

12/

2 times attend a sporting event – professional or other.

1/

2/

1 visit to amusement park.

(note when done)

1 visit to museum.

(note when done)

8 times just enjoy each other and being home – play together.

1/

2/

3/

4/

5/

6/

7/

8/

Have dinner together at home or out depending on the schedule.

Note dates done.

Relax and enjoy the evening together.

Note dates done

Goal: Pay off vacation trip for summer.

Tasks: Divide balance by 3.

Make 3 payments one at the start of each month.

1/

2/

3/

Faith

Goal: Read my daily devotional book every morning and the scripture that goes with it.

Tasks: Get up 30 minutes early each day.

Read, pray and relax with God's Word.

(note on calendar days done, or put calendar in here)

Health

Goal: Walk 200 miles

Tasks: Target minimum walk of 2 miles a day.

Walk 3 miles on weekends or days where you have extra time.

Make sure 1 mile at a time for rain and days unable to make it.

1/   Month one – track total miles walked

2/   Month two – track totals miles walked in month

Add two months together

3/   Month three – track totals miles walked in month

Add all 3 months together

Other

Assignment:

Ok, so there you have the definition.

There you have an example.

Now you need to do this for your tasks, add the measurements.

Key: remember what I show you is an example of how to do it.

Some on you are very detailed people, others of you are not.

You need to track, but you need to track in a method that works for you.

The above works, but you might have to adjust it somewhat.

The key is to measure.

If you don't measure, you don't know if you did it.

Also, you need to celebrate your successes as you achieve them.

Chapter 6 - Accountability

Chapter Objective: Define and write your accountability process.

Render more service than that for which you are paid and you will soon be paid for more than you render.

Napoleon Hill

You are pumped up and ready to roll.

Excited.

Planning this has been hard work, but it is done.

Congratulate yourself.

You did great.

Remember, celebration is important.

Now all you have to do is execute it and you will be successful.

True, but?

Have you been here before?

With other systems and processes?

Pumped up and ready to roll only to see it not happen?

The next thing you need is an accountability partner.

Someone who will keep you on track.

Someone to meet with you weekly and say – how are you doing?

What is working and why?

What is not work, why and how to we get it working?

Not your friend.

Not a nice guy or girl.

Actually, the tougher they are the better.

But who knows best in this area?

You do.

You know how you are.

You know what will work for you and what will not.

But understand, you cannot keep yourself accountable at the level you need to be a superstar. You can be good, even great, but to be extra-ordinary – you need a helper.

If you are one of those people who are not easy to keep on track and do not like to be accountable to anyone – get over it.

You goal is to be extra-ordinary

You cannot get there without an accountability partner.

Get on.

Find a person that will work for you.

I hate CFO's

Sorry if that is your title but I have had some history

And some bad stories.

However, I also know that they are a very necessary piece of running, building and growing a business.

But when I hire a CFO, they have to meet certain conditions that work for me.

Never would I limit their input nor their help.?

But always they would know that I am running the show and their job is to help me.

They are never in charge.

Same with your accountability partner.

You are in charge.

Their job is to show you what you are doing wrong.

And to get you to do something about it.

If you ignore them, then why are they there?

If they are your friend, then they will never be able to do the job, forget it.

I know, I am talking in circles.

But finding this person is critical to your success.

You cannot do it alone.

Take it from one who has tried.

Get over it.

Define what you need in this person and go find them.

It will help your process greatly.

They can be free or paid.

Sometimes paid is better because they have a job to do and have to keep you in line.

I do this for some people, but I am expensive.

Their function is simple this.

1/   Make sure you fill out the weekly accountability sheet.

2/   Take time to meet with them for 30 minutes (can be virtual or live)

        I actually like virtual better – it takes less time and has less social

3/   Don't cut them off.

4/   Listen to them.

5/   Be honest and no covering up.

6/   Take their advice

7/   Go away, mad or not it is ok.

8/   Do what you said you would

9/   If you are not going to listen – then replace them.

But if they are telling you what you don't like, they might just be the right person.

10/   Watch your success factor go up exponentially.

Just like the CFO I hate.

But my business is rocking because of the things he/she tells me that really help me.

Be a leader.

Chapter 7 - Weekly Process:

Chapter Objective: Build your weekly plan.

The major difference between a big shot and a little shot is this:

The big shot is just a little shot who kept on shooting.

Zig Ziglar

Now that you understand what you want to accomplish over the next 90 days, it is time for you to look at this week.

Every week before Monday morning, you need to do what we are going to call, the weekly process.

I do it Sunday afternoons late because that works the best for me.

Some people do it before they close out Friday and some Saturday.

It doesn't matter when as long as it is before Sunday is over.

Because on Sunday night you have to do the Monday daily process.

To do the Monday daily process you need the weekly process done.

The objective in this step is to determine what you are going to do this week.

We start, however, with a review of how we did last week.

This means looking at last weeks scheduled process and review.

What did we get done, what can we celebrate?

What didn't we get done?

What worked?

What didn't work?

What makes you proud?

What makes you unhappy?

You need to feel it.

You need to understand from it and learn.

So many times, we forget to take time to understand.

It is called lessons learned.

This is a very important step.

Also, if there are things you didn't get done that you still need to do (sometimes they just are not important any longer), move them to the next week.

See the attached planning spreadsheet to help you organize this.

Next you need to make a list of what you are going to do this week.

We have a worksheet which we recommend for this process.

But you can do it just on a piece of paper if that works better for you.

First thing to do is list the things that are already on your calendar for this week.

You list the task and then in brackets () put the day and time. (use "R" for Thursday and "A" for Saturday).

If I have an appointment with Jack on Wednesday at 10 to coach him.

I list Jack coaching(w10) as a task for the week.

Now because that will require preparation and follow up, I could also list those as tasks.

On my list I would have

> Jack coaching(w10)
>
> Prepare Jack
>
> Write up Jack

Any task that has a scheduled date/time, put the on as part of the task name.

Now continue on your calendar putting all your appointments on this list.

Use ("R" for Thursday and "A" for Saturday)

Next to each of these tasks you should also put a letter that stands for the 90-day goals that it relates to.

Let's go back to our 90-day goal sheet example and assign one or more letters to each task. If the task is the same area you can reuse it.

Business

S Generate 200K in income   Sales

O Implement the new ABC CRM system. Operations

S Hire a full-time sales rep.   Sales

Personal

PPD Read 3 books
    Personal/Professional Development

Fam Play golf twice a month.   Family (playing
with son)

Financial

F Pay off credit card 123.   Financial

Home

HC Get deck painted.
   House/car

HC Hire person to mow the lawn and get them started.
   House/car

Family

Fam   Spend Sunday's with my family doing things together.   Family

F   Pay off vacation trip for summer.
Financial

Faith

M   Read my daily devotional book every morning and the scripture that goes with it.

    Ministry

Health

PPD   Walk 200 miles   Personal
Professional Development

Other

Then create what I call a cheat sheet

S   Sales

O   Operations

PPD   Personal/Professional Development

Fam   Family

F   Financial

HC   House/car

M   Ministry

As an example, my list would have these 3 tasks and they would be assigned.

S   Jack coaching(w10)

S   Prepare Jack

S   Write up Jack

Because each of these tasks relate to S or in my case selling.

If you cannot find a category on your 90-day plan then ask yourself first, why am I doing this?

Is it necessary?

If it is necessary, then you can put it into General or go back and review your goals, perhaps you forgot something.

You can also have two goals with the same category letter.

I did that with the revenue and hiring the sales person because both are critical to sales.

You will need the first couple of 90 days to get this in order, but after that you should be fine.

Here is my list of tasks from the sample plan we put together.

You can see what I selected to work on this week because they have an x next to them.

Goals with Tasks:

Business

Goal: Generate 200K in income

Tasks:

X   Execute 12 interviews for the weekly podcast.

X   Do a Facebook live training session every week.

Spend $500 a month on Facebook advertising.

Do 4 emails a month focused on selling courses.

Add 500 people a month to the email list funnel.

X   Schedule and hold two 1v1 meetings a week with prospective clients.

X   Send articles to 1 publication a week

X   Send out 10 speaking requests a week

Do 2 emails about free courses a month

X   Write every day for 1 hour

Put together plan for new sales rep

Manage new sales rep's work

Goal: Implement the new ABC CRM system.

Tasks:

X   Set up the system, get all generic data for set up loaded.

        Load all existing client and prospect data into the new system.

        Train all team members on the system.

        Begin using the system for daily sales activity by 45 days in this period.

        Answer questions and build a FAQ document.

        Build a ticks to help you work faster.

        Get the sales team trained on the process.

        Get the sales team using the system.

Goal: Hire a full-time sales rep.

Tasks:

X   Put the ad out on the website and social media

X   Put the word out to people we know that we are looking.

        Review the resumes.

        Schedule phone interviews, 15 minutes with all people we want to look at.

        Schedule in person interviews with all those that pass the first test.

Define our expectations of the sales rep

Ask them about their expectations of the company.

Share what we expect.

Do personality testing

Make offer if we have viable candidate, if not, go back to step one.

Hire rep

Begin training process in our methods and process.

Team up with existing rep

Get them ready to hit hard in the next 90 days – put their 90 day plan together.

Personal

Goal: Read 3 books

Tasks:

X   Find and acquire 3 books to read.

X   Read 20 minutes everyday.

Goal: Play golf twice a month.

Tasks:

X   Schedule golf at start of each month.

         Execute.

Financial

Goal: Pay off credit card 123.

Tasks:

X   Review balance.

X   Divide into 3 pieces

         Pay each month's current bill and the extra piece.

Home

Goal: Get deck painted.

Tasks:

X   Get the paint

         Powerwash the deck.

         Paint the deck.

Goal: Hire person to mow the lawn and get them started.

Tasks:

X   Put word out to friends that I am looking.

X   Review ads

         Call and talk with at least 5 people on the phone.

         Pick 2 best to come out and talk with us.

         Define the expectations we have of them and them of us.

         Hire and get started if one meets our needs.

         Otherwise, go back to step one.

Family

Goal: Spend Sunday's with my family doing things together.

Tasks:

X   Attend church together in the morning.

         2 times attend a sporting event – professional or other.

         1 visit to amusement park.

         1 visit to museum.

X   8 times just enjoy each other and being home – play together.

X   Have dinner together at home or out depending on the schedule.

X   Relax and enjoy the evening together.

Goal: Pay off vacation trip for summer.

Tasks:

X   Divide balance by 3.

X   Make 3 payments one at the start of each month.

Faith

Goal: Read my daily devotional book every morning and the scripture that goes with it.

Tasks:

X   Get up 30 minutes early each day.

X   Read, pray and relax with God's Word.

Health

Goal: Walk 200 miles

Tasks:

X   Target minimum walk of 2 miles a day.

X   Walk 3 miles on weekends or days where you have extra time.

X   Make sure 1 mile at a time for rain and days unable to make it.

Other

Now if you are using the spreadsheet you can sort and copy those with the x

I am just going to copy down the ones I want to work with.

Note also that I replaced the x with the code for that goal and group like pieces together.

Goals with Tasks:

S   Sales

O   Operations

PPD   Personal/Professional Development

Fam   Family

F   Financial

HC   House/car

M   Ministry

S   Execute 12 interviews for the weekly podcast.

S   Do a Facebook live training session every week.

S   Schedule and hold two 1v1 meetings a week with prospective clients.

S   Send articles to 1 publication a week

S   Send out 10 speaking requests a week

S   Write every day for 1 hour

S   Put the ad out on the website and social media – need sales person

S   Put the word out to people we know that we are looking for sales person

o   Set up the system, get all generic data for set up loaded

ppd   Find and acquire 3 books to read.

ppd   Read 20 minutes everyday.

Fam   Schedule golf at start of each month.

F   Review credit card balance.

F   Divide into cc balance into 3 pieces

F   Divide balance on vacation payment by 3.

F   Make vacation payment this week

HC   Get the deck paint

HC   Put word out to friends that I am looking for Grass cutting person

Hc   Review ads for lawncare

Fam   Attend church together in the morning.

Fam   8 times just enjoy each other and being home – play together.

Fam   Have dinner together at home or out depending on the schedule.

Fam   Relax and enjoy the evening together.

m   Get up 30 minutes early each day.

M   Read, pray and relax with God's Word.

PPD   Target minimum walk of 2 miles a day. Walk 3 miles on weekends or days where you have extra time. Make sure 1 mile at a time for rain and days unable to make it.

Amazing, I now have a list the things I need to do this week

I now merge in the appointments from my calendar into the proper category

The example I gave you would go under S

One final point.

There may be some things you thought of that are not on your list, but you now know you need to do them to accomplish your task.

Just add them to the weekly list.

There also may be some general stuff that you need to add.

But what you have now is a list, by category of what you want to get done this week.

What do you think?

I think this is amazing.

It seems like a great deal of work, and initially it might be more than you want to do.

But, if you do it, you will find that in 1 hour a week, you will have a plan and you will accomplish so much more.

One more quality check.

Do not be afraid to go back through there now and say – wow, too much.

Then eliminate some of the things you had put in for this week.

Exercise for this section:

Now go to your task list and select those things that you want to work on this week and make a list just like we did in the example above.

Chapter 8 - Daily Process:

Chapter Objective: Build your daily processes each day.

After 30 days in business, Apple was on the verge of being profitable.

Steve Jobs Biography

Now it is time to get down to the daily process.

This is the key that will drive you every day to create and accomplish so much more.

Once you accept this and start doing it, you will be amazed at the results you come home with.

I guarantee it.

If you do what we have laid out, you will be successful. You will blow all the others away.

Success will be yours.

Daily

Write your goals

       Once in am

       Once in pm

       Not the tasks, just the goals.

    I know this is hard.

    I know when you start it seems a bit crazy.

    But it works.

And after a bit, you will have a need to do it.

Note: once you have completed a goal, take it off the list you write daily.

Your list should get smaller and smaller as the 90 days go past.

It only takes 5 minutes and you will be amazed at what it does for you.

Once you do it daily, it becomes a habit and you have to do it.

As you write these, every day ask yourself, what am I going to do on this goal today

Which tasks can on my list should I be doing today?

2/   Daily list of what you are going to do today.

This piece must be done the night before. You need to go through your weekly list and decide what you are going to do today.

Put these things on a daily list.

Do not do this in the morning.

Do it the night before.

You can do it before you stop working for the day, or before you go to bcd.

But do it before you sleep.

The reason is simple.

As you sleep your subconscious mind will think about the things you have to do and will prepare you better to make it happen.

I did not come up with that, it is proven by the experts.

Step 1 is just taking a moment and writing it down.

      1/   Three things you are grateful for today.

      2/   Three things that made you happy today.

      3/   Three things you accomplished well today.

      4/   Anything you learned.

Step 2 is put the list for tomorrow together.

So here is the weekly list from the example above.

Now what I want to do is select what I am going to do today.

I do that by putting an "x" next to the things I want to do today.

This is easier on the spreadsheet, but you can see what I am doing here.

xS   Execute 12 interviews for the weekly podcast.

S   Do a Facebook live training session every week.

xS   Schedule and hold two 1v1 meetings a week with prospective clients.

S   Send articles to 1 publication a week

xS   Send out 10 speaking requests a week

xS   Write every day for 1 hour

xo   Set up the system, get all generic data for set up loaded.

S   Put the ad out on the website and social media – need sales person

S   Put the word out to people we know that we are looking for sales person

xppd   Find and acquire 3 books to read.

xppd   Read 20 minutes everyday.

Fam   Schedule golf at start of each month.

F   Review credit card balance.

F   Divide into cc balance into 3 pieces

HC   Get the deck paint

xHC   Put word out to friends that I am looking for Grass cutting person

Hc   Review ads for lawncare

Fam   Attend church together in the morning.

Fam   8 times just enjoy each other and being home – play together.

xFam   Have dinner together at home or out depending on the schedule.

xFam   Relax and enjoy the evening together.

F   Divide balance on vacation payment by 3.

F   Make vacation payment this week

xm   Get up 30 minutes early each day.

xM   Read, pray and relax with God's Word.

xPPD   Target minimum walk of 2 miles a day. Walk 3 miles on weekends or days where you have extra time. Make sure 1 mile at a time for rain and days unable to make it.

Now I take and create the list of just what I am going to do today.

xS   Execute 12 interviews for the weekly podcast.

xS   Schedule and hold two 1v1 meetings a week with prospective clients.

xS   Send out 10 speaking requests a week

xS   Write for 1 hour

xo   Set up the system, get all generic data for set up loaded.

xppd   Find and acquire 3 books to read.

xppd   Read 20 minutes

xHC   Put word out to friends that I am looking for Grass cutting person

xFam   Have dinner together at home or out depending on the schedule.

xFam   Relax and enjoy the evening together.

xm   Get up 30 minutes early each day.

xM   Read, pray and relax with God's Word.

xPPD   Target minimum walk of 2 miles a day. Walk 3 miles on weekends or days where you have extra time. Make sure 1 mile at a time for rain and days unable to make it.

Now go through there making sure you don't have too much and remove some if you feel you do.

xS   Write every day for 1 hour

       Changed to

xS   Write for 1 hour

If I had a major amount of client work to do today I might have to take something else off.

However, I recommend doing 4 tasks directly related to your business every day.

Now that you have the list, next define what hours you are available today.

I know you are available all day, but maybe not.

I am a big believer in the 5 hours work day which comes from the book authored by Stephan Aarstol, which really talks about limiting the hours of work. Great book to read and one I recommend to you.

But also remember you do want to schedule the other events in your life. Although you may elect to use this only for work, I believe you are missing a great opportunity if you do that.

Now let's take the tasks and put them into when in the day.

500		Read, pray and relax with God's Word
600		Walk 2 miles
630		Write for 1 hour
730		Breakfast
800		Travel to shop
800	1000	Set up the system, get all generic data for set up loaded.
1000	1030	Meeting
1030	1100	Catch up block
1100	1200	Find people for interviews for the weekly podcast.
1200	100	Lunch
100	200	Work on Scheduling 1v1 meetings
200	300	Send out 10 speaking requests
300	330	Catch up block
330	500	Work with team on the system
500	530	travel home
530	630	Have dinner together at home or out depending on the schedule.
630	700	Find and acquire 3 books to read.
700		Put word out to friends that I am looking for Grass

cutting person

730	930	Relax and enjoy the evening together.
930	1000	Prepare Daily Task List for next day
1000		Bed

You now have all you need for the next day.

WOW!

You can see that I built in a couple of 30 minute catch up blocks.

These are to make it real.

You could have more or less, but I think a couple will make it a more real schedule.

Does it always work out this way?

Most times no, but it gets closer and closer all the time.

You will be amazed.

Exercise.

OK, your turn now.

Review your day.

Take your weekly tasks for this week and let's put them into the matrix.

It will again, take some time in the beginning, but as you do it, you will be amazed.

Chapter 9 - Daily Morning Routine

Chapter Objective: Introduce you to a morning process and get you to move forward in building one.

Anything worthy must carry a measure of pain.

John Adams

I do a great deal of listening to Podcasts. One of my favorites which I really encourage all of you to listen to is Entrepreneur on Fire with JLD. He has, by the time you read this, interviewed around 2000 entrepreneurs. WOW!

One thing I hear from great majority of them is that they have a morning routine. Is it amazing how time after time he will ask one of the keys to the success of his guests and the answer usually is, "I have a morning routine and I live by it." Or "Before I had it, I could not get things done."

Yes, I know most of us hate to get up in the morning.

Get over it.

Successful people get up early.

JLD the host of the show has a morning routine.

And so does Manny.

In fact, what I want to do right here is encourage each of you who doesn't already have a morning routine, to develop one.

It will help you greatly on this road to success.

But, what is a morning routine and what does it involve.

How do I put it together?

Why is it so important?

The first reason is that it works – look at the successful entrepreneurs out there, they have one.

Second, the morning is the most important time of the day, period. I don't care if you are not a morning person, I was not either. What you get done before noon is so critical to your success. Successful people get more due before 9AM than most people get done all day.

What does your morning routine look like, what do you do?

They all look different.

Some have exercise.

Some have meditation.

Some have reading.

Some people walk, run or jog.

Some people do yoga.

Some people write.

Some work on the key pieces of their business.

Each of us may have a different process, but the process works for us and without it our day is just not going to produce the results we need it to.

Here is mine just so you get a feel for what I am talking about.

1/   Exercise 25 minutes (pushups, sits up, squats, curls, lifts, bench)

2/   Hydrate 4 glasses of water

3/   Teeth, face, shave

4/   Read and study God's word.

5/   Motivational note to my children and others

6/   Write my goals

7/   Breakfast

8/   Walk 2 miles

9/   Check bank balances and activity

About 2 ½ hours.

Then I write for 1 hour

Then I start the rest of my day based on my plan.

The only pieces not on weekend are usually walk, exercise and bank.

But the rest, happen 7 days a week.

I have been doing some form of this for over 30 years now.

It works.

So, part of your journey is to develop a routine for when you get up.

It can be much simpler and shorter than mine, but the key is to commit.

Mine was much shorter and simper once, but now I understand how important it is and I also have made more time in my life for what really matters to me.

You might just get up and meditate for 15 minutes

You might just read for ½ hour.

You might run 3-5 miles.

But you need to have a morning routine to be successful.

Plain and simple.

Don't just bush it off.

This is critical to the process and to making it work.

Exercise:

Now I want you to create your own morning routine.

It can be 30 minutes or 3 hours.

I suggest starting small.

But write it down here and then begin doing it.

You will be amazed.

If you want to share it with me, just email it to me at

Manny@MannyNowak.com

Subject: (Name) morning routine.

Chapter 10 - Final Word From Coach Manny

Chapter Objective: Final words and get rolling.

We must in every walk of life believe we can succeed, or by definition, we already have failed.

Jon Huntsman

There you have it.

All you need to create great success in your life.

It is work.

Initially it will be much more work than you want to deal with.

Get over it

Get started.

Get started today.

This book will help you to be so much more successful.

When you look at things 90 days at a time it is like magic.

The reason I asked you to read the entire book before taking action is because it is implemented in a different order. Here is how I want you to proceed forward.

1/   First, build and work your morning routine until you get it down, Chapter 9. Go back, read the chapter again and then do it.

To help you, here is the actual training video we use in the course.

Video: https://youtu.be/Xa8lihuEVxl

2/   Next, I want you to build a daily schedule, chapter 8. Go back, read the chapter again and then do it. You must first learn to manage your day before you can go to a week or a 90-day period. It is a little harder and more difficult because you have not built the other processes yet, but do it. List the things you want to do tomorrow and schedule them. Do this for the number of days it takes until you feel you understand it, you execute it and you are having success. You are doing what you said you would.

That could be 2 days or it could be 2 months or anything in between, but get it working first before you go to the weekly process.

3/   Next, I want you to build the weekly schedule, chapter 7. Go back and read the chapter again and then do it. You have to adjust a little because you do not have a 90 days plan yet, but do it. Make a list of what you need to do, just like chapter 7 says but you have to do it from what you know not from the 90-day process. But you can do this because you know what you have to do and you can use your calendar.

Again, it could take a couple of weeks or a couple of months.

But get the weekly and daily and morning processes down. Even if you never do any more than this, if you stop right there, you will be years ahead of most people. But I want you do to it all.

4/   Now go back to the beginning and build the long-term and 90-day plans. Your first. Because you have already worked and understand the rest of the process, you will now be totally up and running. It will amaze you. But more, you will be getting so much more done.

Call, email, PM or text me any questions at this point, you are ready to roll.

Note: you can also go to our website and purchase the 90 Days to Your Success Course.

This course has all the material in the book, but it is enhanced with the video training courses and the spreadsheets you need to make this easier to implement.

To learn more, click here.

http://coachmanny.com/90-days-to-your-success/

Special Bonus:

Here is a sample of the video training you get in the course.

Please watch and learn.

Video: http://youtu.be/Xa8lihuEVxl

ABOUT THE AUTHOR

Manny Nowak is an Executive Business Consultant, Author of 10 books, and Profession Speaker to business owners organizations all over the country.

The central theme of his message is: "that we learn to be great leaders from the failures we have gone through, reviewed, understood and learned from." By learning from our failures, we can maximize our potential. By learning from our failures, we take control of our fear and move forward. Manny is committed to development of outstanding leaders throughout the world.

What makes Coach Manny different? Simply put, "he has done it." He does not talk and teach theory.

Manny has built companies both his own and others. He knows what it takes to make it happen. His tools and processes help to bring clear, simple, easy to use applicable principles to you in all you do. If you cannot apply what you learn today, what good is it?

He produces a weekly newsletter and video that goes to thousands of people all over the world. A teaching piece to help you get better and better in your work, life, faith and family.

Thank YOU!

Much success to you in all you do.

Thank you for reading this book.

Please give us a review on Amazon.

And please share your experiences and your successes with me.

I would love to hear how you do.

Thanks,

Coach Manny Nowak

Here is my connection data and some of the tools you can work with today.

Website:

www.CoachManny.com

Facebook Page:

www.facebook.com/manny.nowak

Linkedin Profile:

www.linkedin.com/in/mannynowak/

Products:

90 Days to Your Success

http://coachmanny.com/90-days-to-your-success/

Double Your Sales Course

http://coachmanny.com/double-your-sales/

Coach Manny's private Facebook group: The Entrepreneur Toolbox

http://coachmanny.com/coach-mannys-inner-circle/

Hire Manny to speak at Your next event:

http://coachmanny.com/need-a-speaker/

Interested in having Manny as your coach?

http://coachmanny.com/business-results-coaching-2/

Other Books by Coach Manny

http://coachmanny.com/books-by-coach-manny/

Free Courses from Coach Manny:

http://coachmanny.com/free-courses-from-coach-manny/